FOREWORD

It is with great pleasure that I recommend to you this short guide to the rejuvenated Broughton House and Garden. Ever since the E A Hornel Trustees transferred the property to The National Trust for Scotland in 1997, we have been working extremely hard to bring forward a programme of survival and conservation to ensure the preservation of this wonderful house and its unique collections.

We are now able to re-present the property after nearly two years' closure. During this time our project team and the contractors have completed substantial repairs, installed state-of-the-art environmental controls and undertaken a vast amount of conservation to the collections. Indeed so prolific a collector was Hornel that collections conservation will continue for a further year!

None of this work would have possible without the support and financial assistance of the Heritage Lottery Fund; Historic Scotland; Scottish Enterprise Dumfries & Galloway; donations from individual landfill site operators under the Landfill Tax Credit Scheme, administered through Solway Heritage; Members' Centres and Friends Groups; charitable trusts; foundations; corporate sponsors; and individuals who supported the Broughton House Museum Appeal. I note also a personal thank you to all the many dedicated and enthusiastic volunteers who have been so generous with their time and ongoing support, an absolutely vital component of this project.

Our guiding principle has been to preserve and conserve as much of the original fabric and surface textures as possible, intervening with the new only where necessary. For the first time we are able to invite you behind the scenes, to areas of Hornel's house not previously on public view, which give greater insight to the life and passions of this great artist, gardener, collector and bibliophile. I do hope you enjoy the result of our efforts.

David J McAllister
Director, South Region, The National Trust for Scotland

E A Hornel in the gallery at Broughton House about 1930

Broughton House is a treasury of art, impeccable taste, and irresistible effects. It is the external efflorescence of the soul of the painter whose joyous creations have profoundly enlarged the aesthetic vision of the race.

James Shaw Simpson, *Scottish Country Life*, 1916

THE MAN; HIS HOUSE; AND ITS COLLECTIONS

BROUGHTON HOUSE NESTLES IN THE ANCIENT HEART OF THE PICTURESQUE TOWN OF KIRKCUDBRIGHT, WHICH SITS ON THE LEFT BANK OF THE RIVER DEE IN DUMFRIES AND GALLOWAY, IN SOUTH-WEST SCOTLAND. FROM 1901 TO 1933, THE HOUSE BECAME THE HOME AND WORKPLACE OF EDWARD ATKINSON HORNEL (1864-1933), A NATIVE OF KIRKCUDBRIGHT, AND ONE OF THE MOST INNOVATIVE AND SUCCESSFUL ARTISTS TO LIVE AND WORK IN SCOTLAND IN THE LATE NINETEENTH AND EARLY TWENTIETH CENTURIES.

Bessie MacNicol, Portrait of E A Hornel, 1896.
The conservation of this painting was sponsored by Patrick Bourne

Hornel's reputation as a painter originates with the famous group of progressive artists who came to be known as the Glasgow Boys. Hornel was one of the group's youngest members and, from the late 1880s, he and his great friend George Henry led the Boys towards an experimental, decorative style of painting, characterised by a use of brilliant colour and pattern, and an interest in symbolism. Between 1889 and 1895, Hornel and Henry created some of the most original and controversial pictures to be produced by any artists in Scotland at this period. A nineteen-month journey to Japan in 1893-4 resulted in some of Hornel's most important work, and established his reputation as one of Scotland's rising artist stars.

Hornel's ambition to push the boundaries of artistic convention was evident from an early age. Exasperated with the rigid training offered by the Edinburgh School of Art, he fled, aged nineteen, to the Royal Academy of Fine Arts in Antwerp, where he flourished under its dynamic Professor of Painting, Charles Verlat. Throughout his life, Hornel exhibited a taste for travel and foreign cultures, visiting far-flung destinations such as Japan (in 1893-4, and again in 1920-1), Ceylon (Sri Lanka), Australia, Burma (Myanmar), Singapore and Hong Kong. It is perhaps all the more extraordinary, therefore, that – unlike so many of his peers – Hornel was never lured by the bright lights of Edinburgh or London, but remained happily rooted in his beloved home town of Kirkcudbright. On his return from Antwerp in 1885, he moved back into his family home at 18 High Street, and thereafter settled in Kirkcudbright for the rest of his life, helping to cultivate the town's budding artists' colony.

Left: Hornel, Tizzy (seated left) and other family members in the studio, pre-1910

We still have a lot to learn about the development and functioning of Hornel's studio. The room appears to have made use of reclaimed materials from earlier buildings. The Gothic-arched window frames in this photograph were removed around 1910, when the Gallery was added. The source of these architectural features is not yet known, but it is possible that they were salvaged from an ecclesiastical site

An appreciation of Hornel's deep sense of belonging to Kirkcudbright is fundamental to an understanding of the man, his art, and of Broughton House. Hornel's ancestors had lived in Kirkcudbright since the late 1500s. In the eighteenth and nineteenth centuries the Hornel family, including Hornel's father William, were involved in the boot and shoe-making trade, for which the town was celebrated. In 1856, Hornel's parents emigrated to Australia, where Hornel was born in 1864, at Bacchus Marsh in Victoria. However, he had little opportunity to develop any cultural identity with Australia, for his family returned to Kirkcudbright in 1866, when he was just a toddler.

Hornel's father died in 1879, leaving behind his wife, Ann, and eight children, including five daughters, of whom only one was ever to marry. Hornel's decision to settle in Kirkcudbright as an adult was therefore bound up with a sense of duty: throughout his life he assumed the role as the patriarchal head of the family. Over the years, he was to develop a passionate interest in the history of the town and the local area. This passion doubtless evolved out of a desire to uphold and reinforce his family's long-held links with the ancient burgh, and was to find expression in his paintings, in his involvement with community affairs, and in the furnishing of his home, which included the creation of a remarkable library.

By the time Hornel came to acquire Broughton House in 1901, he had already reached the peak of his creativity as an artist. Towards the late 1890s, he tempered the overtly modern style of his paintings, to increase their public appeal and saleability. Turning to the attractive countryside around Kirkcudbright, such as Brighouse Bay on the Solway Firth, he generated a new repertoire of subjects, themed on children playing in pretty rural settings. This change of tack heralded a marked improvement in Hornel's finances, and coincided with his purchase of Broughton House, one of the grandest private properties on Kirkcudbright's High Street.

Broughton House takes its name from Alexander Murray of Broughton and Cally, a Provost of Kirkcudbright and local landowner, who purchased the property in 1740. During the eighteenth and nineteenth centuries, Broughton House was occupied by a succession of local worthies, including bailies, ministers and the 5th Earl of Selkirk. The house's long association with distinguished figures from Kirkcudbright's past would have greatly attracted Hornel, whose social status was on the rise. Importantly, however, the house offered the potential for a purpose-built studio. Before the sale of the house was even completed, Hornel commissioned the Glasgow architect John Keppie to design a large, top-lit extension to the rear of the property. This room was to become the hub of Hornel's painting activity for the next thirty years.

Left: the gallery c1910

Bottom left: the hall, c1916. The hall of Broughton House was densely displayed with objects from Hornel's collections, including oriental and early English blue and white china, pewter and antiquarian curios

Bottom right: Hornel's library in the 1950s. This was the original drawing room of Broughton House. After the building of the gallery in 1910, this room was taken over by Hornel as his library and lined out with bookcases

Opposite page: E A Hornel, **Girls Picking Blue Flax**, 1917. Scenes of young girls in picturesque Galloway landscapes formed the mainstay of Hornel's paintings in the latter half of his career

Hornel made a number of other alterations to Broughton House, culminating in 1910 in the addition of a magnificent gallery on the principal floor. Designed by Keppie, the gallery performed a dual function as a showroom for Hornel's paintings, and the house's main sitting room. Clad in luxurious mahogany, and incorporating casts after the Parthenon frieze, a monumental stone fireplace, and a canopy of skylights emulating classical coffered ceilings, the Broughton House gallery stands as a grandiose statement of Hornel's arrival as an established, solvent artist. For all its interior ostentation, however, the gallery is discreetly invisible from the exterior of Broughton House. Both inside and out, Hornel took great care not to compromise the property's old world charms, skilfully harmonising his modern alterations and choice of furnishing with the building's existing period features.

To the rear of the property, hidden from passers-by behind a high boundary wall, Broughton's other unexpected glory is a delightful garden, which slopes down to the banks of the Dee. The garden was to become an increasing preoccupation for Hornel in his later life. Inspired by his trips to Japan, it developed into a work of art in its own right, interweaving colourful planting with ponds, a rock garden and stepping-stones, punctuated by sculptural features, such as sundials, and architectural fragments lovingly salvaged from local sites.

Hornel's devotion to Kirkcudbright and the local area found its greatest outlet in an overwhelming passion for collecting books, which gripped him in his mid-fifties and preoccupied him for the rest of his life. In 1919 he embarked on a mission with his bibliophile friend Thomas Fraser, to create for Kirkcudbright 'the perfect local library'. This public-spirited endeavour was given legal weight in 1920, when Hornel drew up a Trust Deed, in which he laid down that, after his death and that of his elder sister Elizabeth (Tizzy), Broughton House 'with all its furnishings and my library, curios, works of art and other articles therein should be preserved for the purposes of a Public Art Gallery and Library for the benefit of the inhabitants of Kirkcudbright and visitors thereto.'

Over the next thirteen years he pursued this vision with a determination and vigour that bordered on obsession. By the time of his death in 1933, the library had grown to over 15,000 volumes and spilled into every room of the house. His collection focused specifically on material relating to the Dumfries and Galloway area (including an exceptionally important body of work connected with the Scottish bard Robert Burns). It embraced books, manuscripts, drawings, photographs and printed ephemera, as well as archaeological finds and antiquarian curios. This extraordinary local history collection jostled for elbow room with Hornel's own artwork and personal possessions, which included hundreds of photographs gathered during his foreign travels, studio props and a mass of oriental blue and white china and Scottish pewter.

Hornel's vision for a public art gallery was not conceived as a monument to his own career as an artist. Indeed, the Broughton House collections are in no way representative of Hornel's artistic achievements. Most of the works in the collection date to the later period of his career. Regrettably, there are few examples of the avant-garde paintings of his youthful heyday, the greatest of which are now in major public art collections, such as Glasgow Museums and Art Galleries and the Walker Art Gallery in Liverpool. From the outset, he envisaged both the library and gallery as housing 'living', rather than static, collections, which would be added to as funds and opportunities allowed. Since Hornel's death, numerous books and works of art, including pictures by other local artists in his circle, have entered Broughton House.

Hornel died in 1933. He was outlived by his sister, Tizzy, who, as her brother's constant companion for over thirty years, was granted life rent of the house and its contents. On her death in 1950, the administration of Broughton House was conferred upon a body of Trustees, made up of high-ranking local public officials. For over forty years, the Hornel Trust ably managed Broughton House, with invaluable support from the Friends of Broughton House and Garden. Increasing pressure on finances, however, capped by a fire in the gallery in 1992, prompted the Hornel Trust to invite The National Trust for Scotland to help manage the house and its collections, and finally, in 1997, to assume full ownership of the property.

THE CONSERVATION PROJECT: HIGHLIGHTS

FROM THE LATE 1990S, THE NATIONAL TRUST FOR SCOTLAND BEGAN A CAMPAIGN TO UNDERTAKE A MAJOR PROGRAMME OF CONSERVATION ON BROUGHTON HOUSE AND ITS CONTENTS. IN 2002, THIS FINALLY CAME TO FRUITION WITH THE GENEROUS AWARD OF £1 MILLION FROM THE HERITAGE LOTTERY FUND.

A fundamental objective of the conservation project has been to increase existing knowledge of Broughton House and Garden, and its heritage significance. Thorough observation and recording is an essential part of this process, and a detailed archaeological survey, carried out at the start of the project, provided a baseline for subsequent investigation and conservation decisions. The survey highlighted the complex development of the property which, in its current form, combines two houses (numbers 12 and 10 High Street), and three gardens (numbers 10, 12 and half of 14). Several building phases are evident, the most significant being a major remodelling of the house c1820, involving the addition of elegant bow windows, and Hornel's own alterations in the early twentieth century.

The principal block of Broughton House (No.12) was built on the site of an earlier tenement. A datestone, incorporated during a later period into the masonry of the gallery walls, indicates that construction on the principal block was completed around 1734. The main façade is set back from the common line of the High Street by a raised entrance courtyard, which is supported on barrel-vaulted cellars at street level. The cellars are the only surviving structures from the first house on the site, and can now be viewed by the public, along with the later kitchen, pantries and service routes, which have been newly opened up to visitors as a result of the conservation project.

Right: isometric views of Broughton House, indicating likely building phases (Kirkdale Archaeology Report 1998)

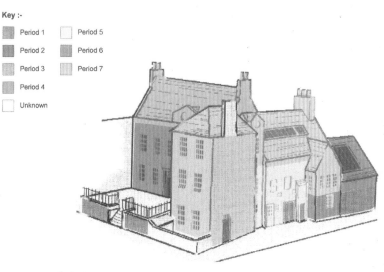

Key :-

Period 1		Period 5	
Period 2		Period 6	
Period 3		Period 7	
Period 4			
Unknown			

Fig. 87 : Phased Isometric View 1

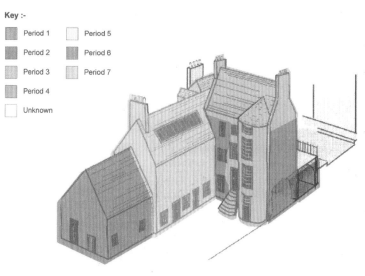

Key :-

Period 1		Period 5	
Period 2		Period 6	
Period 3		Period 7	
Period 4			
Unknown			

Fig. 88 : Phased Isometric View 2

The architectural relationship of the cellars to the later building formed the nub of some of the most serious long-standing damp problems at Broughton House. High levels of humidity caused by water ingress presented a significant risk to the interiors and collections, in particular the books and archives. Extensive measures have been taken to rectify these problems, with the introduction of waterproof membranes and new damp courses, together with a conservation heating system to help regulate the internal environment.

Weatherproofing of the building has been bolstered by coating the exterior stonework with a new, protective limewash – a decision supported by historic photographs of Broughton House, which indicate that the walls were limewashed during Hornel's ownership. The colour was identified by analysing samples from surviving pigment on the house's sheltered elevations. Throughout the project, great emphasis has been placed on reinstating and preserving original finishes. During the second half of the twentieth century, Broughton House underwent several redecorating programmes, which obliterated most of Hornel's decorative schemes and dramatically altered the tonal balance of the interiors. Thanks to painstaking work by teams of conservators, large areas of historic wall coverings have now been revealed throughout the property. The most exciting discoveries include a pillar-box red paper with a bold foliage design in the new exhibition room, and a charming leaf-pattern stencil in the reading room.

Above top: interior of gallery, looking west towards the chimneypiece, showing boarded protection – an illustration of the extensive measures taken to protect original finishes during the contract works

Above: a view of the cellars beneath the raised entrance courtyard

Left: Fiona Butterfield, Paper Conservator, stabilising the historic wallpaper in the new exhibition room

Background image: detail of historic wallpaper in new exhibition room

Previously out-of-bounds due to structural weakness in the floors, the exhibition and reading rooms, together with Hornel's library, all on the first floor of the property, make up the most significant addition to the new visitor route. The opening up of these rooms allows the Trust to adequately interpret the library and archives for the first time, and to provide modern facilities for private study. The desire to improve access – both physical and intellectual – has driven many of the Trust's decisions throughout the conservation programme. The project has provided an opportunity to introduce a lift to the lower and upper ground floors, so that the principal rooms are now available to wheelchair users, and to thoroughly revise the interpretation and educational provision at the property.

Preventative conservation lies at the very heart of the Trust's purpose. Tremendous effort has been directed at introducing measures to improve the property's defences against major risks such as fire, theft, light damage and poor storage. Broughton House is only the second National Trust for Scotland building – after Newhailes – to have a full fire suppression system installed. The confined nature of the interior spaces at Broughton demanded unique solutions, in order to accommodate the necessary pipe work with minimal interruption to the building fabric. Every window in the property has been protected with film that filters out harmful UV light, and fitted with blinds to further reduce light levels. The introduction of blinds to the enormous skylights in the gallery and studio presented a particular challenge, requiring, in the gallery, the installation of a complex motorised system. The library and archives now benefit from modern, conservation-standard storage facilities, including roller-racking shelf units, and refrigerated storage for the collection's thousands of glass-plate negatives and photographs, which include images from Hornel's foreign travels and pictures taken as compositional aids for his paintings.

Remedial conservation, that is, the stabilisation and repair of objects that have already sustained damage, can offer immediately gratifying results. A core aim of the project was to assess the condition of every object in the collections, and to treat as a matter of priority all artefacts that were actively deteriorating. These included two of the star exhibits in the Broughton House painting collections: Hornel's *Man in a Red Tunic*, painted in 1885 while he was studying in Antwerp, and Bessie MacNicol's iconic portrait of Hornel, painted in 1896 when he was at the height of his artistic career. The paint surface of both these pictures was found to be alarmingly fragile, requiring the works to be consolidated and fully relined. During cleaning, the Hornel portrait was discovered to be surprisingly soiled and the gentle removal of the surface dirt has enhanced the quality of MacNicol's vibrant brushwork.

Above top: view of roof space above the gallery, showing new blinds on skylight windows

Above: the main plant for the new fire suppression system, ingeniously concealed within the cellars of Broughton House

Left: E A Hornel, *Man in a Red Tunic*, oil on canvas, 1885

Far left: *Man in a Red Tunic* during relining. The painting was presented to Broughton House by Mrs Louise Walmsley, a Life Member of the Friends of Broughton House, in 1986. Its conservation was sponsored by the Friends of Broughton House and Garden

Unexpected discoveries are always part of the fun and challenge of a conservation project. Among the most important findings at Broughton House was a large painted wall hanging, which was brought back by Hornel from his first trip to Japan in 1893-4. This hanging inspired the decorative backdrop to MacNicol's portrait of the artist, but had suffered extensive damage. Now conserved, this treasured possession can again take its place in Hornel's home.

Above left: detail of Japanese hanging before conservation, showing lifting paint layers and areas of loss

Above right: Helen Creasy, Paper Conservator, working on Japanese hanging

9

Top left: installation in progress of the waterproof membrane under raised entrance courtyard. The exisiting flagstones were recorded, referenced and relaid in their original positions

Top middle: exhibition room: structural repairs to the floor in progress. During the twentieth century, many alterations were carried out at Broughton House to accommodate modern services such as electricity and central heating. In this room, the joists had been so heavily notched to receive cabling and pipework, that over the years the stability of the floor was compromised, causing a dangerous deflection. In order to keep as much of the original fabric as possible, the joists have been strengthened with steel, rather than replaced, and a new secondary floor installed, to rectify the alarming slope

Top right: the introduction of preventative conservation measures in progress, showing the installation of the pipework and wiring for the fire suppression and environmental heating systems

Above left: view of new reading room, showing historic stencilling during conservation

Above middle: Danielle Sheard, Historic Scotland Structural Wall Painting Intern, helping with conservation of the stencilling in the new reading room. This picture illustrates the labour-intensive nature of revealing historic finishes

Above right: view of main stair, midway through conservation, showing removal of white emulsion paint from the historic wallpaper

Opposite page top: detail of the cast of the Parthenon frieze from the gallery

Opposite page bottom: Mo Bingham, Project Conservator for Broughton House, cleaning the canopy of the gallery fireplace with brush and vacuum suction

THE FUTURE

The reopening of Broughton House on 1 April 2005 marks a new beginning in the property's long history. The choice of day is significant, for it was on 1 April 1950 that Hornel's sister, Tizzy, died, signalling the inauguration of the Hornel Trust and the start of Broughton House's new role as a public museum and art gallery. Fifty-five years on, the 1st April again ushers in a new, positive chapter in the story of the house. The Trust's conservation project, however, is not over. For every question that has been answered about the House and its collections, another has been raised. And Hornel's remarkable garden, which has patiently sat out the recent attention lavished on the building, unquestionably deserves future investment. Improved access to library and archives will, it is hoped, generate new study and research that will continually enlighten the Trust's understanding, presentation and care of this most special of properties.

Above left: Hornel and Tizzy in Broughton House garden in the early 1930s. Hornel's garden was one of his chief passions, and is a rare example in Scotland of an artist-designed garden. He planted the magnificent climbing hydrangea that covers the studio wall, the magnolia near the summer-house, the large cherry trees and yucca by the pool, and the wisterias throughout the garden

Above right: the network of paths and pools is also believed to date from Hornel's time

Below right: view of studio wall showing some of the many sundials and sculptural fragments throughout the garden

Opposite page: view of garden from top floor of Broughton House, showing the studio extension to right-hand side with the River Dee behind